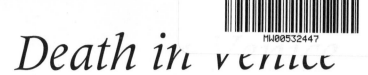

Death in Venice

AN OPERA IN TWO ACTS

Libretto by
MYFANWY PIPER

based on the short story by
THOMAS MANN

set to music by
BENJAMIN BRITTEN
Op.88

FABER *ff* MUSIC

Libretto © 1973 by Faber Music Ltd
First published in 1973 by Faber Music Ltd
This edition published in 1993 by Faber Music Ltd
3 Queen Square, London WC1N 3AU
Cover illustration by John Piper
Printed in England by Caligraving Ltd

ISBN 0 571 51453 7

The first performance of 'Death in Venice' was given by the
English Opera Group at the Maltings, Snape, on 16th June 1973,
as part of the twenty-sixth Aldeburgh Festival

CAST

Singers:

GUSTAV VON ASCHENBACH, a novelist	*tenor*
THE TRAVELLER	*bass-baritone*

who also sings THE ELDERLY FOP
               THE OLD GONDOLIER
               THE HOTEL MANAGER
               THE HOTEL BARBER
               THE LEADER OF THE PLAYERS
               THE VOICE OF DIONYSUS

THE VOICE OF APOLLO	*counter-tenor*
HOTEL PORTER	*tenor*
STRAWBERRY SELLER	*soprano*
ENGLISH CLERK in a travel bureau	*baritone*
TWO STROLLING PLAYERS	*soprano and tenor*

CHORUS *(generally)*:
    Youths and girls, hotel guests and waiters, gondoliers and boatmen, street vendors and touts, citizens of Venice, choir in St Mark's, followers of Dionysus

Dancers:

    The Polish mother
    TADZIO, her son
    Her two daughters
    Their governess
    JASCHIU, Tadzio's friend

Other boys and girls, Strolling Players, beach attendants.

CONTENTS

Death in Venice

ACT ONE

SCENE 1: Munich

(ASCHENBACH is walking in the suburbs of Munich on a spring evening.)

ASCHENBACH   My mind beats on
and no words come.
Taxing, tiring,
unyielding, unproductive –
my mind beats on.
No sleep restores me.

I, Aschenbach,
famous as a master-writer,
successful, honoured,
self-discipline my strength,
routine the order of my days,
imagination servant of my will

My mind beats on,
why am I now at a loss?

I reject the words called forth by passion
I suspect the easy judgement of the heart –
now passion itself has left me
and delight in fastidious choice.

My mind beats on,
and I am at an end.
O tender leaves and tardy spring refresh me!

(He stops before the entrance to a cemetery.)

How solitary it is here –
the silent graveyard,
and the silent dead.

(He notices the texts on the facade of the mortuary chapel.)

CHORUS	'They enter into the house of the Lord'.
ASCHENBACH	Yes! From the black rectangular hole in the ground.
CHORUS	'May light everlasting shine upon them'.
ASCHENBACH	Light everlasting? Would that the light of inspiration had not left me.

(He is suddenly aware of the TRAVELLER standing on the steps of the chapel. They stare at each other.)

Who's that? A foreigner, a traveller no doubt –
from beyond the Alps by his looks.
How he stares: a rude, insolent fellow.
I won't, don't want to notice him.

(He turns away, sunk in thoughts called up by the TRAVELLER.)

TRAVELLER	Marvels unfold! A wilderness, swollen with fearful growth, monstrous and thick, and heady flowers crowd in the streaming marsh. Trees, distorted as a dream, drop naked roots into a glass-green pool, where float great milk-white blooms and at the stagnant edge huge birds stand hunched and motionless.
ASCHENBACH	Strange – strange hallucination, inexplicable longing.
TRAVELLER	See! in the knotted bamboo grove (O terror and delight) a sudden predatory gleam, the crouching tiger's eyes.
⎡ ASCHENBACH	What is this urge that fills my tired heart, a thirst, a leaping, wild unrest, a deep desire!
⎣ TRAVELLER	Marvels unfold! No boundaries hold you, Go, travel to the South. Great poets before you Have listened to its voice.

(*ASCHENBACH looks for the TRAVELLER, but he is nowhere to be seen.*)

ASCHENBACH   Gone, he's gone, as suddenly as he came –
the traveller from beyond the Alps.

Should I go too beyond the mountains?
Should I let impulse be my guide?
Should I give up the fruitless struggle with the word?

(*He takes from his pocket a small book, the symbol of his novelist's trade.*)

I have always kept a close watch over my
development as a writer, over my behaviour as a
man. Should I now, without thought, break my habit,
my summer of work in the mountains, to holiday in
the warm and lovely south? The break can be
justified of course by this growing fatigue, that no one
must suspect and that I must not betray by any sign
of flagging inspiration. Yes, it can be justified – but the
truth is that it has been precipitated by a sudden
desire for the unknown.

(*He puts his book away.*)

So be it!
I will pursue this freedom
and offer up my days
to the sun and the south.
My ordered soul shall be refreshed at last.

OPTIONAL CUT

SCENE 2: On the boat to Venice

(*Some youths lean over the boat rail and shout to their girl friends on shore.*)

YOUTHS   Hey there, hey there, you!
You come along with us,
come along do!

GIRLS (*on shore*)   Not with you, not very likely, not with you!

ONE YOUTH   Aren't you old enough to leave home?

(*They all laugh.*)

TWO GIRLS   You be quiet!

YOUTHS   'Serenissima, Serenissima'

ONE BOY   Let the girls alone,

| | there are plenty where we're going. |
| ANOTHER | . . . plenty where we're going. |

GIRLS	Look out for the girls over there!
	They'll hook you, they will!
	They'll trap you, they will!
	They'll get you, they will! They will!

ONE YOUTH　　　　Thanks, we can look after ourselves!

(The youths are joined by their friend, the ELDERLY FOP.)

GIRLS	Ho! Here comes young Casanova,
	there, him with the hat.
	He'll make trouble!

ELDERLY FOP	Me Casanova?
	Me make trouble?
	I don't know what trouble is, do I boys?

YOUTHS　　　　Doesn't know what trouble is, does he boys?

ELDERLY FOP *(going up the gangway)*
　　　　　　　　　Come on, cara mia!
　　　　　　　　　We'll be nice to you.

YOUTH　　　　Hi, come back!
(following him)

ELDERLY FOP　　　　Leave me alone, boys!

(They struggle with him and pull him back as the hooter sounds and the boat leaves.)

ELDERLY FOP　　　　I say, we're off! Addio!

YOUTHS *(on boat)*　{ We're off, thank goodness. Addio!
　　　　　　　　　　{ We're off. Hurrah for Serenissima, Addio!

GIRLS *(on shore)*　{ You're off! Too late! Be careful do! Addio!
　　　　　　　　　　{ They're off, good riddance too. Addio!

(The ELDERLY FOP stops the 'Addios' and starts the song.)

ELDERLY FOP	We'll meet in the Piazza,
and YOUTHS	The flags will be flying,
	And outside San Marco
	The girls we'll be eyeing.

(ASCHENBACH comes on to the deck.)

ELDERLY FOP　　　　Hush boys, quiet!
　　　　　　　　　We have a noble companion on board.

YOUTHS	We'll sit in the Piazza,
	The band will be playing,
	But inside San Marco
	They're singing and praying.
ELDERLY FOP	Greetings, Conte!
(to ASCHENBACH)	Bound for Serenissima I'm sure.

(ASCHENBACH starts as he sees he is not young, but elderly, rouged and wrinkled.)

ASCHENBACH	Why, he's old!
	He's not young at all.
ELDERLY FOP	But you look doubtful?
	Pray don't change your mind, you won't regret it!
	Venice – an excellent choice,
	you'll find everything you're wanting –
	won't he, boys?
(laughs)	
YOUTHS	The bells of San Marco
	Call us to our duty
	But I'll leave the Piazza
	And follow my beauty.

(They run off.)

ASCHENBACH	Ugh! How can they bear that counterfeit
	that young-old horror.
	A wretched lot, a wretched boat.

(A STEWARD comes forward with a chair.)

STEWARD	Do you want a chair, Signore?
ASCHENBACH	Yes, put it there, away from the young men.
(to himself)	What romantic notion
	made me want to come by sea?

(The STEWARD puts the chair down and ASCHENBACH settles himself.)

YOUTHS *(off)*	'Serenissima'
ASCHENBACH	Low-lying clouds, unending grey
YOUTHS *(off)*	'Serenissima'
ASCHENBACH	Beneath the sombre dome
	the empty plain of the sea.

(He dozes.)

(The ELDERLY FOP crosses in front of ASCHENBACH.)

YOUTHS *(off)*	'Row us over to Serenissima'
ELDERLY FOP	Hush boys, the Conte is dreaming!
	Dreaming of love and Serenissima.

(He goes off.)

(ASCHENBACH gets up and looks towards the shore of Venice now visible.)

YOUTHS *(off)*	'Serenissima'
ASCHENBACH	Where is the welcome
	that my Venice always gave me?

(The boat arrives and the ELDERLY FOP and the YOUTHS, by now rather drunk, come running on.)

ELDERLY FOP *and* YOUTHS	Here we are, here we are!
ELDERLY FOP	Wait for me, I'm coming too
	I want my beauty, Hurrah!
YOUTHS	Hurrah for the Piazza
	The pride of the city
	All hail to San Marco
	Hurrah for my beauty!

(They all rush on shore, followed slowly by ASCHENBACH.)

ELDERLY FOP *(to ASCHENBACH)*	Au revoir, Conte!
	Pray keep us in mind
	and, by the way,
	our love to the pretty little darling –
	don't you know!

OVERTURE: Venice

SCENE 3: The journey to the Lido

(ASCHENBACH is in a gondola rowed by the OLD GONDOLIER.)

ASCHENBACH	Ah Serenissima!
	Where should I come but to you
	To soothe and revive me,
	Where but to you,
	To live that magical life
	Between the sea and the city?

	What lies in wait for me here, Ambiguous Venice, Where water is married to stone And passion confuses the senses? Ambiguous Venice.
GONDOLIER *(to himself)*	Passengers must follow Follow where I lead No choice for the living No choice for the dead.

(ASCHENBACH suddenly realises the GONDOLIER is rowing out to the Lido.)

ASCHENBACH *(to GONDOLIER)*	Where is the man going? I want to go to Schiavone.
GONDOLIER	The Signore is going to the Lido.
ASCHENBACH	Yes, by vaporetto.
GONDOLIER	The Signore cannot go by vaporetto, the vaporetto does not take baggage.
ASCHENBACH	That is my affair; you will turn round.
GONDOLIER *(to himself)*	Nobody shall bid me I go where I choose I go my own way I have nothing to lose.
ASCHENBACH *(to himself)*	Is it money he's after?
GONDOLIER	The Signore will pay.
ASCHENBACH	I will pay nothing if you do not take me where I want to go.
GONDOLIER	To the Lido.
ASCHENBACH	But not with you.
GONDOLIER	I row you well.
ASCHENBACH *(to himself)*	True, he rows well. I shall leave him alone, go back to my dreams, to the sway of the boat and the indolent lapping waves.
GONDOLIER *(to himself)*	They know how I row them They take what I give

But nobody shall bid me
Not while I live.

(A boatload of boys and girls singing is heard in the distance.)

CHORUS *(off)* Serenissima, Serenissima
Row us over to Serenissima

GIRL	Bride of the sea	BOY	True bride for me
GIRLS	Gossip and stroll	BOY	Eye every girl
GIRL	Choose the right one	BOY	Make her your own
GIRLS	If she won't come	BOYS	Leave her alone
GIRLS	Loiter and play	GIRLS	Tease every boy
BOYS	You play too long	BOY	I'll change my song

BOYS *and* GIRLS Serenissima
Bride of the sea
True bride for me.

(As the boatload comes nearer ASCHENBACH throws them money.)

ALL Mille grazie, Signore.
Tanti auguri.
Addio, addio . . .

(fading away)

GONDOLIER Nobody shall bid me
(to himself) I do what I want to
I'm not out to please.

(The gondola arrives at the Lido quayside. ASCHENBACH gets up and is helped ashore by a BOATMAN and the HOTEL PORTER.)

BOATMAN Buon giorno, Signore. Piano, piano!

PORTER This way, Signore, prego.

ASCHENBACH One moment please, I have not paid the gondolier.

(He turns to pay the OLD GONDOLIER, who has disappeared.)

Why he's gone, gone without his money.

PORTER He made off, Signore,
A bad lot.

BOATMAN He was recognised here,
a bad lot.

PORTER A man we don't trust.

BOATMAN	A man without a licence.
BOTH	But the Signore is lucky,
	he had his gondola ride for nothing.

(ASCHENBACH tips the BOATMAN. The HOTEL PORTER picks up his baggage and carries it off, ASCHENBACH walking slowly behind him.)

ASCHENBACH	Mysterious gondola,
	a different world surrounds you,
	a timeless, legendary world
	of dark, lawless errands
	in the watery night.
	How black a gondola is –
	black, coffin black,
	a vision of death itself
	and the last silent voyage.
	Yes, he rowed me well.
	But he might have done for me,
	rowed me across the Styx
	and I should have faded
	like echoes in the lagoon
	to nothingness.

SCENE 4: The first evening at the hotel

(The HOTEL MANAGER welcomes him.)

| MANAGER | We are delighted to greet the Signore |
| | to our excellent hotel. |

(ASCHENBACH nods.)

| | We trust the Signore had a pleasant journey; |
| | he will have a pleasant sojourn I am sure. |

(ASCHENBACH nods.)

	The Signore was wise to come to the Lido by gondola,
	not so fast as the boat, but pleasanter, far pleasanter.
ASCHENBACH	That was not my intention.
MANAGER	Just so, but a happy chance none the less.
	And here is the room, as you commanded,
	and look Signore, the view!
	The view of the beach from our rooms is superb,

	from this one especially.
ASCHENBACH	Thank you, it will do very well.
MANAGER	And here, Signore, outside your room, but private, unfrequented, you may sit and see the world go by. For men of letters, like the Signore, take pleasure in the contemplation of their fellows –
ASCHENBACH	Thank you.
MANAGER	– for the Signore is well-known in our country.
ASCHENBACH	Thank you, very nice, quite satisfactory.
MANAGER	Prego, egregio Signor von Aschenbach.

(The HOTEL MANAGER bows himself out.)

ASCHENBACH *(with book)*	So I am led to Venice once again – egregio Signor von Aschenbach; the writer who has found a way to reconcile art and honours, the lofty purity of whose style has been officially recognised and who has accepted, even welcomed the austere demands of maturity. Yes, I turned away from the paradox and daring of my youth, renounced bohemianism and sympathy with the outcast soul, to concentrate upon simplicity, beauty, form – upon these all my art is built. Now, in this beautiful, agreeable place, I intend to give myself to the leisured world for a spell. A pleasant journey did he say? The whole experience was odd, unreal, out of normal focus. Was I wrong to come, what is there in store for me here?

(He puts his book away.)

> But there is the sea
> and near by Serenissima
> though the sky is still grey,
> the air heavy, a hint of sirocco.

(He gets up and looks out to the sea and the beach.)

> How I love the sound
> of the long low waves,
> rhythmic upon the sand.

(The HOTEL GUESTS watch their children begin to process before dinner and ASCHENBACH turns to watch them.)

ASCHENBACH	But here the sound is of another kind.
GUESTS *(all)*	The Lido is so charming, is it not.
FRENCH GIRL	Maman, le diner quand sera-t-il servi? Je meurs de faim.
FRENCH MOTHER	Tais-toi, Bérénice c'est assez!
ALL	And this hotel is all that one could wish.
TWO AMERICANS	
FIRST	That was a most interesting excursion.
SECOND	Most interesting.
FIRST	We should have Mario guide us again tomorrow.
SECOND	Mario? Mario!
ALL	And Venice is so close one is not bored beside the sea.
GERMAN FATHER *and* MOTHER	Komm' mein Kindchen, lass' uns hören was die Wellen dir erzählen.*
ALL	One meets one's friends from everywhere – from Warsaw!
A POLISH FATHER *(to his son)*	Jęśli jutro będzie pogoda to pojedziemy na wyspy.*
ALL	and Denmark!
DANISH LADY	Det er så varmt.*
ENGLISH LADY *(replying)*	What was that you said, dear?
ALL	and Moscow!
RUSSIAN NANNY *(to her children)*	Тары–бары–растабары, Снежки белы выпадали, Серы зайцы выбегали, Охотнички выезжали, Ты постой,стой,стой,стой...
RUSSIAN PARENTS *(interrupting her)*	При Маме/Папе надо вести себя прилично! *
ALL	So civilised, quite so. So elegant, quite so, So 'comme il faut', don't you know.
HOTEL PORTER *and* WAITER	Signori! Il ristorante, al vostro servizio.

* *See page 46 for translation*

(All the Guests, repeating their individual phrases, go towards the dining room.)

ASCHENBACH   United in their formal ways
in the ease that wide horizons bring.
Well-mannered murmurs of a large hotel.

(The Polish family (GOVERNESS, two girls and TADZIO) enter. ASCHENBACH notices them.)

ASCHENBACH   Poles, I should think,
Governess, with her children –
a beautiful young creature, the boy.

Surely the soul of Greece
Lies in that bright perfection
A golden look
A timeless air,
Mortal child with more than mortal grace.

(TADZIO's mother comes in. The family gets up, bow and curtsey, and they all move off into the dining-room.)

ASCHENBACH   How does such beauty come about? What mysterious
(with book)   harmony between the individual and the universal
law produces such perfection of form? Would the
child be less good, less valuable as a human being if
he were less beautiful? The fact is that in that
disciplined family, beauty dominates. The severe,
plain little girls must be quiet, demure; the elegant
boy may show off his grace. No doubt Mama with her
fabulous pearls indulges herself in a pampering partial
love – just as I indulge myself in these novelist's
speculations. There is indeed in every artist's nature a
wanton and treacherous proneness to side with
beauty.

SCENE 5: On the beach

(ASCHENBACH and hotel guests)

ASCHENBACH   The wind is from the West
a lazy sea,
the sky overcast,
a stagnant smell from the lagoon.
My temples throb, I cannot work

O Serenissima, be kind,
or I must leave,
just as once I left before.

(A group of children play at beach games. ASCHENBACH watches them.)

(A STRAWBERRY SELLER wanders across the beach. The children stop and watch her.)

STRAWBERRY SELLER	Le bele fragole, La bela, bela ua. Fine strawberries, Signori, fresh today.

(The game continues. The SELLER goes to ASCHENBACH who buys some strawberries.)

STRAWBERRY SELLER	Grassie, Signore . . . Bellissime!
ASCHENBACH	I'll stay, I cannot leave. What can be better than the sea? What can be better than this?
(with book)	Ah, how peaceful to contemplate the sea – immeasurable, unorganised, void. I long to find rest in perfection, and is not this a form of perfection?

(ASCHENBACH raises his head to see TADZIO coming on to the beach.)

Ah here comes Eros – his very self.
I was not mistaken, it is very good.

(A little pantomime of TADZIO's hatred of the Russian family.)

So the little Polish god is proud,
proud like all his race.
He is human after all.
There is a dark side even to perfection.
I like that.

(TADZIO goes and sits down with his family. His friends call him to join them.)

CHORUS *(off)*	Adziù! Adziù!

(He gets up and slowly wanders over to the other boys.)

CHORUS *(off)*	Adziù! Adziù!
ASCHENBACH	What is it they call him, Adziù! Adziù? They call him Adziù!

(Children's games with TADZIO as ringleader. They play in the water. TADZIO runs back wet to his mother.)

CHORUS *(off)*	Adziù! Adziù!
ASCHENBACH	Tadziù, Tadziù! that is it . . .
	from Thaddeus, short for Thaddeus.
	Tadzio.

(TADZIO joins the children again. They acknowledge him as their leader. He then walks back to his mother. She presents him to some of her friends, and he smiles rather self-consciously.)

ASCHENBACH	So, my little beauty,
	you notice when you're noticed,
	do you?
(with book)	As one who strives to create beauty, to liberate from the marble mass of language the slender forms of an art, I might have created him. Perhaps that is why I feel a father's pleasure, a father's warmth in the contemplation of him. Yes, Aschenbach, you have grown reserved, self-sufficient since the death of a wife and marriage of an only daughter – dependent not upon human relationships but upon work, and again – work. How much better to live, not words but beauty, to exist in it, and of it. How much better than my detached and solitary way.

SCENE 6: The foiled departure

(ASCHENBACH crosses to Venice in a gondola.)

GONDOLIER	Aou'! Stagando, aou'!
	Aou'!

(At the landing place, ASCHENBACH gets out and starts walking through the streets. He looks unhappy and uncomfortable. Vendors and beggars cry to him from all sides.)

A GUIDE	Guida, guida! Let me guide the Signore.
	I can find him places he does not know,
	places to delight him.
ASCHENBACH	While this sirocco blows
	Nothing delights me.
	My head is heavy,
	My eyelids ache.
A LACE SELLER	Guardi, Signore, see the beautiful silks and lace.

	Tutto a buon mercato. *(many times repeated)*
A GLASSMAKER	Venga qui, Signore, look at my beautiful glass.
	Tutto a buon mercato. *(many times repeated)*
ASCHENBACH	Foul exhalations rise
	Under the bridges,
	Opress my breathing,
	Dispel my joy.

BEGGAR WOMAN *(with her child)*
        La carità, la carità!
        Il padre is sick,
        the bambini are hungry,
        la carità.

A RESTAURANT	Provi, Signore!
WAITER	Vongole, granseole, aragosta,
	gamberetti, mazanette,
	calamaretti molto buon'.
	Provi, Signore!

BEGGAR WOMAN	La carità,
	il padre is sick,
	bambini hungry,
	la carità.

ASCHENBACH	The rubbish stirs in gusts
	Over the piazzas.

GLASSMAKER	Venga qui, Signore, look at my beautiful glass.
	Tutto a buon mercato. *(many times repeated)*
ASCHENBACH	Every doorway
	Harbours feverish fears.

LACE SELLER	Guardi, Signore, see my beautiful lace.
	Tutto a buon mercato. *(many times repeated)*
ASCHENBACH	O Serenissima,
	I fear you in this mood.

GUIDE	Guida, guida, Signore!
	I can find places you do not know,
	places to delight you.

(ASCHENBACH has now arrived back at the landing stage.)

ASCHENBACH	Enough, I must leave, I must go away.
	Back to the mountains –

and the fresh mountain air.

(He gets into the gondola.)

But where? where shall I go?
I must leave this unfriendly lagoon
horrible, evil, nauseous.
I must go elsewhere,
I must find a clearer sky
a fresher air.

GONDOLIER   Aou'! Aou'!

ANOTHER GONDOLIER *(off stage)*
       Aou'! De longo aou'!

(The gondola arrives at the Lido. ASCHENBACH gets out.)

(Passage of time.)

(ASCHENBACH is revealed in the hotel hall.)

MANAGER   Naturally, Signore, I understand.
       How regrettable, unfortunate.
       We shall be sorry to lose you,
       but of course if the Signore has reasons
       then he must go.

(ASCHENBACH nods.)

       No doubt the Signore will return to us in his own
       good time.

(ASCHENBACH nods.)

       Meanwhile our deepest respects
       and please keep us in mind.
       Arrivederci, Signore!

(ASCHENBACH nods.)

(calling)   Giulio, veni qui.
       The Signore's baggage. Presto.

PORTER   Sì, pronto! Sì, sì.
       It is here.
(to ASCHENBACH) The motor-boat is waiting.

ASCHENBACH   It is too soon,
       you allow too much time,
       I will not be hurried.

| | I will follow by gondola. |
| PORTER | Bene, Signore. |

(He goes off with the baggage.)

| ASCHENBACH | Yes, I must go –
but does it seem fresher this morning?
Can the wind have changed? |

(TADZIO walks through the hall.)

For the last time, Tadziù,
it was too brief, all too brief –
may God bless you.

(TADZIO glances at ASCHENBACH.)

(Passage of time.)

(ASCHENBACH in the gondola.)

| GONDOLIER | Aou'! |

ANOTHER GONDOLIER *(distant)*
Premando aou'!

| ASCHENBACH | Shall I never see these columns rise again?
Never see the marble brows
upon each curving bridge?
O Serenissima!
Why did I yield so quickly to my fears? |

(The gondola arrives in Venice. The HOTEL PORTER comes to the side of the quay and calls to ASCHENBACH.)

PORTER	There you are, Signore, just in time.
ASCHENBACH	You have my baggage?
PORTER	Safe, Signore, gone on the train to Como.
ASCHENBACH	Gone to Como?
That is not where I'm going.
PORTER	Sorry, Signore.
Mi dispiace, Signore.
ASCHENBACH	You must find it – get it back –
Without it, I cannot go.
You understand? I cannot go.
I shall return to the hotel.
Arrange for the baggage to be sent back there.

PORTER   Very good, Signore.
                    In the twinkling of an eye it shall be back.
(calling)   Gondoliere, to the Lido at once!

(The GONDOLIER starts rowing back to the Lido.)

ASCHENBACH   I am become like one of my early heroes, passive in
                    the face of fate. What do I really want? First I am
                    grief-stricken but must go because of the danger to
                    my health, then I am furious because I am forced to
                    return, but secretly I rejoice. Vacillating, irresolute,
                    absurd.

GONDOLIER   Aou'!
(very distant)

ASCHENBACH   The whole experience has been disruptive to my
(continuing)   thoughts and to my work; yet in spite of it I can feel
                    my spirits rise. Often what is called disruptive is not
                    directed against life, but is invigorating, a renewal . . .

(At the hotel the MANAGER greets him)

MANAGER   A thousand apologies to the Signore,
                    I would not have discommoded him for the world.
                    And now the Signore will find the wind
                    is blowing from the healthier quarter,
                    the wind blows sweetly from the east.

(The MANAGER takes ASCHENBACH to his room and opens the window on to the beach.)

                    Now the Signore
                    can holiday at ease,
                    he can enjoy
                    what he thought to have left
                    for ever.

(The MANAGER leaves. ASCHENBACH remains looking wearily out on to the beach. TADZIO, JASCHIU, and a few other boys are seen playing in the distance.)

ASCHENBACH   Ah, Tadzio, the charming Tadzio,
                    that's what it was,
                    that's what made it hard to leave.

(The boys run off. ASCHENBACH lifts his hands in a gesture of acceptance.)

                    So be it. So be it.
                    Here I will stay,

here dedicate my days to the sun
and Apollo himself.

SCENE 7: The Games of Apollo

(The Lido beach. ASCHENBACH is in his chair.)

CHORUS	Beneath a dazzling sky
(HOTEL GUESTS)	The sea rolls silken-white,
	Calm morning hours drift on
	To scented dusk and melting night
	Day after carefree day
	The idle minutes run
	While he transported to the antique world
	Lives in Elysium.
THE VOICE OF	He who loves beauty
APOLLO	Worships me.
	Mine is the spell
	That binds his days.

(TADZIO 'drives' a group of boys on to the beach.)

CHORUS	No boy, but Phoebus of the golden hair
	Driving his horses through the azure sky

(They form a pyramid and TADZIO climbs to the top.)

Mounting his living chariot shoulder high,
Both child and god he lords it in the air.

(The boys dismount.)

No boy, but Phoebus of the golden hair.

VOICE OF APOLLO	Now in my praise
	They tell again
	Olympian tales
	Of rivalry.

(JASCHIU and another boy vie for TADZIO's attention, watched by TADZIO's mother.)

(While the CHORUS sings, the appropriate actions take place. JASCHIU shows off his acrobatic skill, TADZIO imitates him. The other boy tries to attract TADZIO with his skill, the two boys compete. TADZIO is accidentally knocked down. They carry him across to his mother, who comforts him.)

CHORUS	Come, see where Hyacinthus plays
	Basking in Apollo's rays,

Careless sun that gilds his love
With beauty that will fatal prove.
But a rival watches there
With envious pangs too strong to bear.
Jealous Zephyr's angry breath
Guides the blow that brings his death.
Poor broken boy as on the ground you rest
The curled flower springs immortal from your breast.

VOICE OF APOLLO Love that beauty causes
Is frenzy god-inspired
Nearer to the gods
Than sanity.

(Formal solo for TADZIO.)

CHORUS Phaedrus learned what beauty is
From Socrates beneath the tree
Beauty is the only form
Of spirit that our eyes can see
So brings to the outcast soul
Reflections of Divinity.

VOICE OF APOLLO At the feasts of the sun
See my devotees contest
In strength, agility and skill
  The body's praise.

(The boys compete in a variety of sports.)

(1 Running)

CHORUS First, the race!
Run, run,
get ready go,
foot by foot,
outpace one another,
with flashing forms
legs, thighs, working arms.

(TADZIO is first.)

(2 Long jump)

Next, to the pit.
Try your skill
turn by turn

24

heaving breath –
Go!
Springing high
gather limbs
time the moment –
Go!
Now release
shooting forward
legs and arms
flinging forth
skim, and land
with thudding heel.
Go!

(TADZIO has jumped furthest.)

(3 Discus throwing)

Now, the throw!
Young discobolus
tensing body bent
weighs the swelling stone
firm upon the hand
swinging back and up
gathering all his force
arching wider still
hurling now,
hurling the discus.
Young discobolus!

(TADZIO has thrown furthest.)

(4 Javelin throwing)

On tip-toe rise!
Up and over
graceful turn and drop
higher each one
the heavens attempt
triumphant flying,
free in weightless flight.
Yet to the earth at last
the shaft is bound.

(TADZIO has thrown furthest.)

(5 Wrestling)

> For skill and strength
> this is the final test!
> Measure to fight,
> face your man
> forehead to forehead
> fist to fist
> limbs coiled round limbs
> panting with strain
> tear apart and close again
> immobile now – tensing, tensing!
> Panther-like, a shoulder throw.

(TADZIO is winner of the Pentathlon.)

CHORUS   Who is the victor?
Tadzio has won.
Crown him with olive!

(TADZIO comes forward; the boys dance round him.)

Tadzio has won,
Tadzio is victor.   *(many times repeated)*

VOICE OF APOLLO   Praise,
Praise my power,
Beauty is the mirror of spirit.

(The HOTEL GUESTS and all the children retreat to the distance (the chorus still singing) leaving TADZIO alone. ASCHENBACH rises and comes forward, very excited.)

ASCHENBACH   The boy, Tadzio, shall inspire me.
His pure lines shall form my style.
The power of beauty sets me free
I will write what the world waits for
rejoicing in his presence.

When thought becomes feeling, feeling thought . . .

When the mind bows low before beauty . . .

When nature perceives the ecstatic moment . . .

When genius leaves contemplation for one moment
of reality . . .

Then Eros is in the word.

(TADZIO, sauntering, approaches ASCHENBACH.)

> Ah Tadzio, the victor, the admiration of all,
> I must say well done.
> I must speak to him,
> we will become friends,
> it is easy, nothing more natural.

(TADZIO passes ASCHENBACH who turns away.)

> Too late, I couldn't . . . couldn't do it . . .
> This is frenzy, absurd.
> The heat of the sun must have made me ill.
>
> So longing passes back and forth
> between life and the mind.

(TADZIO's mother comes back with her family to collect him. As TADZIO passes ASCHENBACH on the way into the hotel he smiles.)

> Ah, don't smile like that!
> No one should be smiled at like that.

(then realising the truth at last)

> I – love you.

END OF ACT ONE

ACT TWO

ASCHENBACH
(with book)

So, it has come to this. I can find no better description of my state than the hackneyed words 'I love you'. Overcome by beauty I tried, quite simply to use the emotion released for my own creation. What I wrote was good, quite what was expected of me; to the point, yet poignant. But when it was done I felt degraded – as if I had taken part in an orgy.

Then I was moved to put this relationship – if so onesided an affair can be called a relationship – on to a natural footing. I would hail the boy, exchange a few words with him: I couldn't do it. My beating heart and trembling limbs refused to obey my will. So I had to mock myself as the crestfallen lover.

Who really understands the workings of the creative mind? Nonetheless 'so be it'. This 'I love you' must be accepted; ridiculous but sacred too and no, not dishonourable even in these circumstances.

(Passage of time.)

SCENE 8: The Hotel Barber's shop (i)

HOTEL BARBER

Guardate, Signore!
Va bene, Signore?

(ASCHENBACH is revealed in the barber's chair.)

Move the head to the left.
Yes, the weather is idyllic.
Too hot? O, just a trifle.
The hotel guests are fewer?

(The BARBER holds up a mirror.)

Guardate, Signore!
Va bene, Signore?
Your head down, if you please.
But what was that you're saying?
you hear less German?

	Ah! your compatriots are always very careful but so nice.
	Take the von Becks!
	I've tended Herr von Beck for many summers, a splendid head of hair if I may say so, remarkable for someone in his middle years, and such a youthful skin!
	(Guardate, Signore!)
	Each year they spend the summer with us, (va bene, Signore?)
	but now after ten days they have gone, gone back to the cold unwelcoming north.
	(Head up just a little!)
	The Signore is not leaving us?
	He does not fear the sickness, does he?
ASCHENBACH *(sharply)*	Sickness! what sickness?
BARBER	Nothing, I know nothing.
ASCHENBACH	But you mentioned it.
BARBER	It is not important, it is nothing.
ASCHENBACH	You must know what you mean.
BARBER	Take no notice, sir, it is not important.
	You fancy this oil, sir?
	A delectable scent, sir,
	the Signore now takes little interest in such things, I know.
	That is it, Signore.

(ASCHENBACH gets up from the chair.)

Next week at the same time?
Va bene, Signore, egregio Signore.
Prego, prego!

(ASCHENBACH comes forward as the HOTEL BARBER and his chair fade.)

ASCHENBACH   Sickness, what sickness?
More than a malaise from the sirocco?
A sickness to drive people away?

(Passage of time.)

SCENE 9: The pursuit

(ASCHENBACH is crossing to Venice.)

ASCHENBACH   Do I detect a scent?
A sweetish medicinal cleanliness,
overlaying the smell of still canals?

GONDOLIER   Aou'!

ANOTHER GONDOLIER *(off stage)*
Aou'!

(The Gondola stops and ASCHENBACH gets out. There are many people standing about.)

ASCHENBACH   How quiet the city is!
What can they all be looking at?

CITIZENS *(reading from a notice)*   Citizens are advised to take precautions against
infection.
Citizens are warned not to eat shellfish in this
unusually hot season.
Citizens must not use the canal waters for household
purposes.
People are warned . . . warned . . .

ASCHENBACH   warned . . . warned. . .

CITIZENS   Everyone is warned.

ASCHENBACH   What is all this?
The city fathers are seldom so solicitous.

(moving to talk to some shopkeepers)

What is this sweetish smell
that pervades the air, my friends?

SHOPKEEPERS   Scusi?

ASCHENBACH   What are these warnings?

GLASS MAKER   Just a formal precaution, sir.

RESTAURANT WAITER   Police regulations, sir, with which we must conform.

LACE SELLER   The air is sultry, the sirocco blows.

A GUIDE   No, quite unimportant, sir, precautionary –
Let me guide the Signore,
I can find him . . .

ASCHENBACH	Basta! Basta!

(He turns away)

SHOPKEEPERS	Scusi, Signore!
BEGGAR WOMAN *(pursuing him)*	La carità! The bambini are sick.
NEWSPAPER SELLER *(entering)*	La Stampa! Giornali tedeschi . . . Il Mondo! German newspapers . . .
ASCHENBACH	Das Tagblatt, grazie.
NEWSPAPER SELLER	Grazie, Signore . . . La Stampa! Giornali ingelesi . . . Il Mondo! La Stampa! Giornale, giornale . . .

(goes out)

ASCHENBACH *(reading)*	Let me see what my countrymen say. 'Rumours of cholera in Venice officially denied. Rumours of an incipient plague in Venice officially denied.'

Ah, here it is. 'We doubt the good faith of the Venetian City fathers in their refusal to admit to the cases of cholera in the city. German citizens should return as soon as possible.' Ugh! rumours, rumours. They should be silent. The city's secret, growing darker every day, like the secret in my own heart.

(The Polish family appears.)

They must receive no hint.
They must not be told.
They must not leave.

(ASCHENBACH begins following the family.)

And now I cannot let them out of sight,
daily I watch and wander.
Strange times of chance encounters, painful hopes,
and silent communion.

(The family is sitting at a café table in the Piazza. ASCHENBACH sits near them. The café orchestra plays. TADZIO's mother deliberately gets up and places herself between her son and ASCHENBACH.)

(The family leaves and starts walking. ASCHENBACH follows.)

Careful search now leads me to them,

cunning finds him out.

(The family approaches and enters St Mark's.)

My eyes are on him even at his prayer,
incense and sickness mingle in the air.

(ASCHENBACH follows. TADZIO kneels a little apart from the others. ASCHENBACH stands amongst the casual populace away from the family. There is a service going on. Bells.)

CHORUS   Kyrie eleison, Christe eleison.

(TADZIO is aware of ASCHENBACH's presence.)

Christe audi nos, Christe exaudi nos.
Sancte Marce ora pro nobis.

PRIEST   Ite, missa est.

(The service is over, the family leaves. ASCHENBACH follows them down the Merceria.)

ASCHENBACH   When I am near, he knows.
As for me a calm untroubled face
hides a panic fear –
yet am I driven on . . .

(The citizens gradually appear.)

CHORUS   Fewer guests from smart hotels
come to walk about our streets.

ASCHENBACH   Yet am I driven on.

CHORUS   We who live by summer's trade
guard the city's secret.

ASCHENBACH   Yet am I driven on.

CHORUS   There's no danger if we watch
and do as we are told.

ASCHENBACH   Yet am I driven on.

CHORUS   Under a burning sky
The sirocco still blows.

(ASCHENBACH suddenly comes face to face with the family. He bows, raises his hat and turns away.)

ASCHENBACH   O voluptuous days,
O the joy I suffer:
feverish chase,
exquisite fear,
the taste of knowledge,

time gained by silence
while the echoing cries answer
from the labyrinth.

(The family gets into a gondola.)

ASCHENBACH *(calling to a gondolier)*
Follow them!

(He gets into his own gondola and follows them through the canals.)

GONDOLIERS *(in the two boats)*
Aou'! De longo aou'!

THIRD GONDOLIER *(from a distance)*
Aou'!
Chiamate! Aou'!

FIRST *and* SECOND GONDOLIERS
Stagando aou'!

(The family gets out of their gondola. ASCHENBACH follows them.)

ASCHENBACH   Ah, Tadzio, Eros, charmer,
see I am past all fear,
blind to danger,
drunken, powerless,
sunk in the bliss of madness.

(The family enters the hotel, followed by ASCHENBACH.)

Ah, Tadzio, Eros, charmer.

(TADZIO disappears into his bedroom. ASCHENBACH remains some time leaning against the door post. He then slowly goes to his room.)

(Shaken but excited, he calls himself to order.)

ASCHENBACH   Gustav von Aschenbach, what is this path you have
(with book)   taken? What would your forebears say – decent, stern
men, in whose respectable name and under whose
influence you, the artist, made the life of art into a
service, a hero's life of struggle and abstinence?

(he pauses, smiles to himself)

Yes, but when heroes have flourished Eros has
flourished too. It was no shame to them to be
enthralled, rather it brought them praise, it brought
them honour.

SCENE 10: The Strolling Players

(On the terrace outside the hotel after dinner. The HOTEL PORTER and WAITER are ushering the guests.)

⌈ PORTER	This way for the players, Signori!
⌊ WAITER	Please come this way.
⌈ PORTER	A rough lot of course, but you'll enjoy it.
⌊ WAITER	A rough lot.
PORTER	Yes, they come each year; it is the custom.
⌈ *(answering a guest)*	Take your places, Signori.
⌊ WAITER	Take your places, Signori.

(The HOTEL GUESTS take their places.)

GUESTS
> The players are here,
> Where are our places?
> The players are here
> To charm and delight us
> With quips and grimaces,
> With old songs new turned
> With new antics learned
> To please and excite us
> To woo and invite us
> The players are here,
> We're in our places!

(The Strolling Players begin. A boy and a girl come forward: two acrobats mime the instruments (flute and guitar).)

BOY *and* GIRL	O mio carino/mia carina how I need you near me
BOY	Just as the Siren needs the salt sea water
GIRL	Dearest I weep when you're not near to hear me
BOY	And in my veins the blood begins to falter.
BOTH	Better by far if we had met and parted
GIRL	I knew the Creed, but now I can't get started,
BOY	Can't say the Gloria nor l'Ave Maria,
BOTH	How shall I save my soul, l'anima mia?

(ASCHENBACH takes his place, apart from the other guests.)

> Dearest my life is guided by your beauty

(TADZIO is visible on the terrace.)

	Just as the North star guides the storm-tossed sailor.
BOY	For you forgotten honour work and duty.
BOY *and* GIRL	Carina,/L'anima mia, how shall I save my soul?

(The LEADER OF THE PLAYERS comes forward, an acrobat mimes the trumpet.)

LEADER OF THE PLAYERS	La mia nonna always used to tell me
	'Leave the blondes alone, Sonny –
	Sono tutte vagabonde!'
	La mia mamma always used to tell me
	'Don't you choose brunettes, Sonny –
	Sono tutte traditore!'
	Padre mio always used to tell me
	'Never touch a redhead, Sonny –
	sono tutte . . . sono tutte . . .'
	So I shall never be able to marry –
	Evviva la libertà.

(The LEADER goes among the guests with his hat. ASCHENBACH calls to him.)

ASCHENBACH	A word, please.
LEADER	Signore?

(During this conversation the two acrobats amuse the guests.)

ASCHENBACH	Why are they disinfecting Venice?
LEADER	Orders, just orders.
ASCHENBACH	So there is no plague in Venice?
LEADER	Ha! That's a good one,
	perhaps the sirocco's a plague?
	Or the police, *they* are a plague!
	No, you've got it wrong, Signore,
	it's the heat, the heat and the weather.
	Basta! Basta!

(He tries to go on with his collecting but is intercepted by the HOTEL PORTER)

	Here, hands off!
PORTER	What did you say to the German Signore?
LEADER	Nothing, let go!
PORTER	What did you say?
LEADER	Told him he was talking a lot of nonsense
	that's what I told him.

PORTER	Go on then, they're waiting, and mind you, not a word.

(THE LEADER runs back to the other players and starts the laughing song. ASCHENBACH and TADZIO never join in the laughter.)

LEADER	Fiorir rose in mezo al giasso * e de agosto nevegar.
CHORUS	Ha, ha, ha, ha, How ridiculous you are!
LEADER	Trovar onde in terra ferma e formighe in mezo al mar. *(Chorus)*
	Giovinoto che a na vecia tanti basi ghe vol dar. *(Chorus)*
	Bela tosa che se voia co un vecio maridar. *(Chorus)*
	Oseleto un fià stracheto che sia bon da sifolar.
(to the audience)	What a lot of fools you are!
CHORUS	How ridiculous you are! Ha, ha, ha, ha.

(General laughter, led by the LEADER, grows in intensity until he stops it with a gesture. He then takes the players off amidst applause. The LEADER then starts his antics, ending with a wild gesture. He puts his tongue out at the HOTEL GUESTS, who start leaving uneasily.)

ASCHENBACH *(tenderly)*	Ah, little Tadziù we do not laugh like the others. Does your innocence keep you aloof, or do you look to me for guidance? Do you look to me?

(TADZIO remains quietly for a moment, then leaves. The HOTEL PORTER and WAITER bustle the LEADER off.)

(musing)	So the moments pass; And as they dwindle through the fragile neck Dividing life from death I see them flow

 * See page 46 for translation

As once I saw the thread of sand slip through
My father's hour glass.

(Passage of time.)

A YOUNG ENGLISH CLERK

(from the distance)   One moment, if you please.

(nearer)   One moment, if you please.

SCENE 11: The travel bureau

(A YOUNG ENGLISH CLERK is coping with a crowd of HOTEL GUESTS.)

CLERK	One moment, if you please.
GUESTS *(singly)*	We must go today, no later.
	My ticket please.
CLERK	One moment, if you please.
GUESTS	Information please, it is most urgent.
	Please pay attention to me.
CLERK	One moment, if you please.
GUESTS	Four places in the Wagon-lits for tonight, four places – first class.
	But my dear young man, I said today.
CLERK	One moment, if you please.
GUESTS	A hotel overnight, near the station.
	Called to France – urgent business – I cannot wait – I must go.
	Will you help me please.
CLERK	I'm sorry, Signori, we are closed.

(The HOTEL GUESTS leave in confusion. ASCHENBACH comes forward.)

ASCHENBACH	Young man, why do all these people hurry to leave?
CLERK	The end of the season, sir.
ASCHENBACH	What are these warnings all over the city?
CLERK	The city always takes precautions in this weather.
ASCHENBACH	Is that the truth?

CLERK	Sir, that is what they say, what we are told to believe. But . . .
ASCHENBACH	The truth!
CLERK	In these last years, Asiatic cholera has spread from the delta of the Ganges: to Hindustan, to China, Afghanistan and thence to Persia. They thought it would travel westwards by land, but it came by sea, to the southern ports – Malaga, Palermo . . . Last May, two dead bodies were discovered here in Venice with signs of the plague. It was hushed up. In a week there were ten more – twenty – thirty. A guest from Austria went home and died; hence the reports in the German newspapers. The authorities denied it – the city had never been healthier, they said. Sir, death is at work, the plague is with us. It flourishes, redoubles its powers. It is violent, convulsive, suffocating, few who contract it recover. The Ospedale Civico is full. The traffic to San Michele is continuous. And Sir, the authorities are not moved by scruples, or by international agreements. They fear for their pockets – if there should be panic or blockade . . . Meanwhile the city is demoralised. Crime, drunkenness, murder, organised vice – evil forces are rife. Sir, take my advice. The blockade cannot be far off. Rather than put if off till tomorrow, you would do well to leave today.
ASCHENBACH	Thank you, young man.
CLERK	Good night sir, it is true, every word.

SCENE 12: The Lady of the Pearls

(ASCHENBACH walks up and down agitatedly.)

ASCHENBACH	So it is true, true, more fearful than I thought. I must warn them, warn the lady of the pearls, speak to her now. 'Madame', I will say, 'allow a perfect stranger to give you a warning'.

'Madame', I will say, 'Go away, at once,
you are in danger.
Venice is in the grip of the plague.
Do you not see how everyone is leaving?
You must go too, with your daughters,
and with . . . Tadzio, your son'.
'Madame', I will say, 'Madame'. . .

(The lights go up on the hall of the hotel. TADZIO's mother walks into the hall. ASCHENBACH makes as if to speak to her. She comes right up to him but he turns aside into his room.)

ASCHENBACH *(with book)*	So – I didn't speak! Once again I have failed to make everything decent and above board, missed the opportunity to become myself again, missed the opportunity to regain my reason, my self-possession. But what *is* self-possession? What is reason, moral sense, what is art itself, compared to the rewards of chaos. The city's secret, desperate, disastrous, destroying, is my hope. I will not speak. What if all were dead, and only we two left alive?

SCENE 13: The dream

(A dark stage. ASCHENBACH is faintly discernible asleep.)

DIONYSUS	Receive the stranger god.
APOLLO	No! Reject the abyss.
DIONYSUS	Do not turn away from life.
APOLLO	No! Abjure the knowledge that forgives.
DIONYSUS	Do not refuse the mysteries.
APOLLO	No! Love reason, beauty, form.
DIONYSUS	He who denies the god, denies his nature.
APOLLO	No! Be ruled by me and by my laws.
DIONYSUS	Come! Beat on the drums.
APOLLO	No!
DIONYSUS	Stumble in the reeling dance.
APOLLO *(fading)*	No!
DIONYSUS	Goad the beasts with garlanded staves,

	seize their horns,
	ride into the throng.
	Behold the sacrifice!
APOLLO *(distant)*	I go, I go now.

(The FOLLOWERS OF DIONYSUS appear, dancing.)

FOLLOWERS	Aa-oo! Aa-oo!
DIONYSUS	Taste it, taste the sacrifice.
	Join the worshippers,
	embrace, laugh, cry,
	to honour the god
	I am he!
FOLLOWERS	Aa-oo! Aa-oo!

(The Dionysiac dance reaches a climax and slowly fades.)

ASCHENBACH *(in his sleep)*	Aa-oo! Aa-oo!

(He suddenly awakes.)

(spoken)	It is true, it is all true.
	I can fall no further.
	O the taste of knowledge
	Let the gods do what they will with me.

SCENE 14: The empty beach

(ASCHENBACH slowly moves to his chair on the beach where TADZIO and a few friends are mooning about. They begin a desultory game. It breaks off. They begin another, but soon run off.)

ASCHENBACH	Do what you will with me!

SCENE 15: The Hotel Barber's shop (ii)

(ASCHENBACH is revealed in the chair and the HOTEL BARBER is attending him.)

BARBER	Yes! a very wise decision, if I may say so.
	One should not neglect oneself in one's middle life.
	Everyone should make a stand against advancing years.

(holding up the mirror)

Guardate, Signore, egregio Signore!

Grey? O just a trifle,
due to lack of interest,
you would not neglect your health? your teeth?
Then why refuse the use of cosmetics?
Nothing ages a man like grey hair,
permit me to aid it just a little?

(The BARBER works on his hair with lotions etc.)

Very wise,
magnificent,
all the difference,
va bene, Signore?
Now if we were to tone up the skin?
O just a little, a very little . . .

(The BARBER works on ASCHENBACH's skin.)

Signore, my forte . . .
to bring back the appearance of youth . . .
Va bene, Signore?
Give some brilliance to the eyes–
nothing brightens a face like the eyes!

(The BARBER works on ASCHENBACH's eyes.)

Head back, Signore . . .
quite, quite still . . .
An excellent subject, if I may say so.

(holding up the mirror)

Guardate, Signore! va bene, Signore?
Prego, prego.
A masterpiece, a masterpiece!
Now the Signore can fall in love with a good grace.
Prego, prego,

(accepting ASCHENBACH's tip)

Addio, Signore, egregio Signore!

SCENE 16: The last visit to Venice

(ASCHENBACH (with his new appearance) is seen getting gaily into a gondola.)

ASCHENBACH   Hurrah for the Piazza

The pride of the city
All hail to San Marco
All hail to my beauty

(The gondola stops and ASCHENBACH gets out.)

'the pretty little darling don't you know'.

(He sees the Polish family walking in front of him and starts distractedly following them. TADZIO detaches himself from the rest of his family and waits for ASCHENBACH. He looks full at ASCHENBACH, who turns away.)

ASCHENBACH   He saw me, he saw me, and did not betray me.

(TADZIO joins his family. ASCHENBACH continues to follow but loses sight of them. ASCHENBACH leans exhausted against a well-head. The STRAWBERRY SELLER comes by.)

STRAWBERRY   Le bele fragole,
SELLER   La bela, bela ua,
                 Fine strawberries.

(ASCHENBACH buys some fruit.)

Grassie tante a voi, Signore.

(She goes out singing.)

Signore, fresh today.

ASCHENBACH   Ugh, they are soft, musty, over-ripe!

(He sits down, tired and ill.)

Chaos, chaos and sickness.
What if all were dead
and only we two left alive?
O Aschenbach . . .
Famous as a master . . .
Self-discipline . . . your strength . . .
All folly, all pretence –
O perilous sweetness
the wisdom poets crave.
Socrates knew, Socrates told us.

Does beauty lead to wisdom, Phaedrus?
Yes, but through the senses.
Can poets take this way then
For senses lead to passion, Phaedrus.
Passion leads to knowledge

Knowledge to forgiveness
To compassion with the abyss.
Should we then reject it, Phaedrus,
The wisdom poets crave,
Seeking only form and pure detachment
Simplicity and discipline?
But this is beauty, Phaedrus,
Discovered through the senses
And senses lead to passion, Phaedrus
And passion to the abyss.

And now, Phaedrus, I will go.
But you stay here
and when your eyes no longer see me,
then you go too.

(Passage of time.)

SCENE 17: The departure

(The Hotel Hall leading to the beach. The HOTEL MANAGER is standing waiting. The HOTEL PORTER is fussing around.)

MANAGER
The wind still blows from the land,
the air is not good, it is hot and unnatural.
The time of politeness and welcome
to our excellent hotel is over.

PORTER *(gaily)*
First one goes,
then another goes – è capo?
Soon we shall be all alone – è capo?

MANAGER
Be silent!
Where is the baggage of the lady of the pearls?
Were you not told to bring it down?

PORTER
First one goes,
then another goes,
then five go – è vero, capo?

MANAGER
Begone!

(The HOTEL PORTER goes off.)

MANAGER
When guests arrive at my splendid hotel
I welcome them,

I show them the view.
And when they go,
by choice or chance,
I'm here to say addio!

PORTER *(returning with baggage)*
First one goes,
now they all go.

(He puts the baggage down.)

And the writing gentleman?

MANAGER   Be silent –
who comes and goes is my affair.

(ASCHENBACH comes in wearily. He looks at the baggage.)

Buon giorno, Signor von Aschenbach.

ASCHENBACH   More departures?

MANAGER   Signore, it is the time of departure.

ASCHENBACH   Our Polish friends?

MANAGER   Precisely, Signore,
the lady and her family
now return to their home
in the cold, cold north
beyond the mountains.

ASCHENBACH   When?

MANAGER   After luncheon, to be sure.

(ASCHENBACH nods.)

Yes, Signor Von Aschenbach
the season comes to an end,
our work is nearly done.
No doubt the Signore
will be leaving us soon?
We must all lose
what we think to enjoy the most.

(The HOTEL MANAGER watches ASCHENBACH go out to the deserted beach. He goes to his usual chair. TADZIO, JASCHIU, a few other boys, and TADZIO's sisters come on to the beach. TADZIO and JASCHIU start a game together; the other children watch. The game becomes rougher with JASCHIU dominating. The other children become

frightened. JASCHIU gets TADZIO down: he kneels on his back. The children cry out. JASCHIU presses TADZIO's face into the sand. The other children run off.)

ASCHENBACH   Ah, no!
(trying to get up)

(JASCHIU suddenly lets TADZIO go and runs off. TADZIO slowly gets up as he is called.)

CHORUS *(off)*   Adziù! Adziù! Adziù!

ASCHENBACH   Tadziù!

(At a clear beckon from TADZIO, ASCHENBACH slumps in his chair. TADZIO continues his walk far out to sea.)

END OF THE OPERA

TRANSLATIONS

Page 15
GERMAN FATHER   Come my child, tell us what the waves are saying.
and MOTHER

A POLISH FATHER   If tomorrow is fine then we will go to the islands.

DANISH LADY   It is so hot!

The RUSSIAN NANNY's song is a nonsense rhyme.

RUSSIAN PARENTS   In Mummy's/Daddy's presence one must behave
properly!

Page 36
Translation of the Laughing Song

Do roses flower in the midst of ice.
Does snow fall in August.
(Chorus)

Are there waves upon dry land,
or ants in the middle of the sea.
(Chorus)

Does a young man want
to give an old woman kisses.
(Chorus)

Does a pretty girl wish
to marry an old man.
(Chorus)

Can a tired bird whistle.
(Chorus)